JAZZ
A VOLUME OF POETRY

Chika Agbayi

Copyright © 2021 by Chika Agbayi

All rights reserved. No part of this publication may be reproduced, distributed, or transmitted in any form or by any means, including photocopying, recording, or other electronic or mechanical methods, without the prior written permission of the publisher, except in the case brief quotations embodied in critical reviews and other noncommercial uses permitted by copyright law.

ISBN: 978-1-954341-67-8 (Paperback)

The views expressed in this book are solely those of the author and do not necessarily reflect the views of the publisher, and the publisher hereby disclaims any responsibility for them.

Writers' Branding
1800-608-6550
www.writersbranding.com
orders@writersbranding.com

Contents

SECTION ONE: THOUGHTS ON POETRY 1

    I KNOW THESE POEMS 2
    APPLE VOICE 3
    WILD POEMS 4
    GOD AND HIS SILENT POEMS 5
    SUNRISE, SUNSET 6
    SHRINE OF POEMS 7
    SURVIVORS 8

SECTION TWO: MOTIVATIONAL 9

    TREE OF LEGACY 10
    FAITH 11
    PRAYER TO LIFE 12
    A TOWN CHRISTENED FUTURE 13
    TOUGH LIFE 14
    THREE STEPS OF LIFE 15
    HUMBLE STAR 16
    GUTS 17
    CROSSROADS OF DESTINY 18
    A PLACE IN THE FUTURE 19

SECTION THREE: SPARKS OF TRUTH 20

    SOUL TRAVEL 21
    GOLDEN BIRTH 22
    JOURNEY 23
    THE FAR COUNTRY 24
    WEEP NOT FOR THE DEAD 25
    BAD AND HARD 26
    A RUNNING LIFE 27
    GOOD BYE, DEAR BROTHER 28

SECTION FOUR: NIGERIA: IN THE MIDST OF MADNESS....... 29

    THE POLITICAL RAPISTS 30
    A GHASTLY FUTURE 31
    PARADISE OF DECEIT 33
    BEFORE THE COURT OF CONSCIENCE 34

SECTION FIVE: CHAOS 35

    DELUSION 36
    ARRIVAL AND DEPARTURE 37
    LOVERS IN PARADISE 38
    MEMORIES OF WAR 39
    NIGHT IS AN ACCESSORY 40
    WHY?.. 41

SECTION SIX: LOVE, LIFE, AND THE CELESTIAL 42

    SCHOOL OF LIFE 43
    THE SWEET ABSOLUTE 44
    SUN-WORSHIP 45
    MAD SUN.. 46
    WORSHIP 47
    EYES THAT BECKONED 48
    HISTORY 49
    ASHES TO ASHES, DUST TO DUST 50
    SIGHT BEYOND SIGHT 51
    THE URGE HAS REFUSED TO DIE (1).................... 52
    THE URGE HAS REFUSED TO DIE (2) 53
    A CACHE OF TRICKS 54
    JAZZ... 55
    UNEARTHED BLISS.. 56
    MY NIGHTS AND A NIGHTINGALE 57
    EPILOGUE 58

ABOUT THE AUTHOR 59

ONE
THOUGHTS ON POETRY

For me, as for many people, poetry is a way of expressing our feelings, especially such strong emotions as love, hope, joy, aversion, disenchantment. In making possible a catharsis, poetry enables us to be fully human.

I KNOW THESE POEMS

Before my pen
Kissed the paper,
Left its life
As poetry,
I knew you.

As my eyes walk
Guided by my thought
On this shiny creative path
I know you.

I am your God, your creator.
You are my creation.
In my pen lies your future.
I know you.

I made you
In the image
And likeness
Of pure thought.

These lines had life
Before you were conceived
In the womb of my mind,
Birthed on these plain pages.

I have known these poems before.

APPLE VOICE

When the voice of
Poetry calls at twilight
I romance my pen without remorse
And stone my sleep with solid words.

It calls still.
Still I see the moonlight
In dance of joy.
Little stars shine their applause.

The voice of poetry floods the night.
Subtle rays fall off moon's waist.
The pen speaks in different tongues
To a defenceless plain paper,
Like an artist's busy brush
Crying upon a white canvass.

I am your disciple
Ready to obey your apple voice.

WILD POEMS

Wild Poems
Crowd my mind.
They are like the waters of a dam
Straining for freedom.
Look at them matching down
The path of my soul
Chanting war songs
Seeking calm
On these pages.

GOD AND HIS SILENT POEMS

The ocean
Calm and collected
Deep with blue
Prides itself
For being bottomless.

Deserts,
Too bald for weeds,
Enjoy romancing fingers of the sun.

Mountains –
Daunting peaks pointing to God with humility
Eternally crippled by desire to walk
Into the dazzling heavens.

The wind as it hurries by
Knows the forests must prostrate.
And when earth is thirsty and dry
We wait for the waters from the sky.

These – God's silent poems –
Written on the pages of eternity.

SUNRISE, SUNSET

As the sun rises in my mind,
Fresh ideas detonate
The lonely wind.
Each time it sets,
Insane memories
Unearth chaos.

SHRINE OF POEMS

Bless me, dear God
And let me not muse,

Lost in the labyrinths
Of my creative ability.

Let not my thoughts
Plod in the dark world of negligence.

Guard me against
The tutelage of ignorance.

Bless me, please,
Great God of Poetry.

Make me the priest
In your shrine of poems.

SURVIVORS

The sea, the sea.
The sea of words rage
In the hallowed earth of my mind.

Precious boats of living poems,
In the violence,
Pray not to capsize.

Survivors will sit on the shore
Hoping for a safe delivery
On the pages of forever.

TWO

MOTIVATIONAL

More likely as not, at some point in our lives we have had challenges which we thought were greater than ourselves, but we came out triumphant and, hopefully, realized how limitless we are as souls.

Every one of us has been, or will be, ushered into such moments by life. May these poems help you sail through when life begins to teach some important lessons.

TREE OF LEGACY

I do not care how long I stay here,
But for the legacy I planted
To be nurtured by history.

Let posterity pluck
Stainless fruits of wisdom
From this legacy tree.

FAITH

As a gale, life
Left my dreams in pieces.
Faith, the healer,
Has begun to mould another.

PRAYER TO LIFE

Hear me, O! Life,
For God has kept mute.
Cuddle me in your citadel of love
And throw an arrogant and blinding fire
At the hate out there.

Forgive me for wishful thinking.
Forgive me for musing in vain.
Make my life indelible
On the bare flesh of history.

Crown my brow with wisdom.
Pride me with humility.
Wreathe me with peace profound.
Walk me down this narrow road.
Bring me into the broad future fulfilled.
Take me to the edge of the earth
And, blissfully, I will be transformed.

A TOWN CHRISTENED FUTURE

Let's fling yesterday's fears
Into the jungle of dead disappointment
And sail our canoe of courage
Serenely
Into the wide straits
That glow in hues that glee.

This murky era
Shall be filtered out
Like dusk at dawn.

At dawn
An orange sun
Pretty nude
Hangs above, shy
Peeping through clear spaces
Between palm fronds
In the heart of a scintillating town
Called Future
Where we shall quench our thirst for comfort
As we drink from the stream of success.

TOUGH LIFE

I am poor
Life is rough, tough.
But a day shall come
With gold and diamond
And slabs of love
I will mould a home
Perfectly adorned with peace and quiet,
Living like a king, dignified,
Without fear of pestilence
Giving thanks to none but God
Never out of job, fulfilled
In the labour of my heart and hand.

THREE STEPS OF LIFE

The past:
Dark, dead.

Now:
Peace comes with a sun yet tender, half-awake.

The future:
I see the sun alight on the shore of fulfilment.

HUMBLE STAR

Life's sharp edges
Gave me indelible scars
In order to mould
A humble star.

GUTS

When my past
Strikes with the sharp machete
Of painful memories
My guts blunt it.
And I am no soothsayer,
But, at present,
I see light streaming into my future.

CROSSROADS OF DESTINY

At the crossroads of destiny
History blows the flute of wisdom.

Sounds fall into the wind
Like raindrops on our souls.

He who foresees his destiny
Is like a hero amongst heroes.

But be not petrified, even as
Sad tales seek attention
In the gloomy side of life.

Be patient
For the patient man
Eats the fleshy fish.

Let the sun warm the sky
The moon to colour each night
And the rain to soften the earth.

Be not dubious in your dealings
For justice will be your shield.

Move, comrades,
Let's match on the paths of our destiny.

A PLACE IN THE FUTURE

Every man is soul,
A spark of God.
And every soul's
Is a profound destiny.

Every man now living
Has lived before.
As for every death
The certainty of resurrection.

Every turbulent sea
Has had its moments of calm.
Like every prostitute
A virgin once.

For every nightmare
Is a soothing daydream.
And every night
Has its day.

Every dark life
Has a dazzling light
Waiting to burst upon it
Somewhere in the future.

THREE
SPARKS OF TRUTH

Our purpose on earth is to attain the fullest awareness of our spiritual divinity. Consequently, earth is not soul's true home, but only a place where soul may reside awhile on its journey back to God, The Sweet Absolute. And death is not the end of life. In fact, soul is indestructible, eternal.

SOUL TRAVEL

Soul's tomb I left.
Veiled behind me the earth.
Onto a lawn which glowed I sailed
Searching for the depth of death.

I sailed on a wind so gentle
And swam in a light so subtle.
The birds blue
Before a glass-like cloud
They glided, magnificent.

No sun or moon to blaze, or shine.
Stars never stared.
The scene alighted
In silk-soft hues.

Like a fast-flying slug
The notion struck my mind:
Earth is the prison yard of the universe!

GOLDEN BIRTH

If my soul will rise when I die
Then death is the real birth.
I will be so light,
Floating on the white love of God
Into Its heavens of
Brilliant light and amiable silences.
There lives Timelessness.
Roses ever young,
Ever smiling.
Souls shining.
Darkness not known.
Pure love worshiped.

If death is the real birth
And it is soul's re-birth
Then it is a golden birth.

JOURNEY

We leave as dazzling souls.
Sailing through the bliss
In the tranquil wind
We come to earth.

We bond with other souls.
We seek the fragrance of mortality.
We wear the cloth of humans
To learn to be humane.

When it's time to move on
We wail in fury
Cry and curse
Till we grow weary.

But the journey must go on
The quest
For brighter lights
Deeper truths.

THE FAR COUNTRY

Mr. Kwete was a seeker of truth, a lover of God.
He knew death as a close friend.
He saw simplicity as great beauty.

Mr. Kwete slept one night.
The morning arrived with a young sun
Found him cold and stiff.

Mr. Kwete was said to be dead.
Family and friends wept and mourned.
A dear friend was dead and gone.

But, believe it or not,
Somewhere in the far country
Mr. Kwete still lives, not dead.

WEEP NOT FOR THE DEAD

The requiem mass is on.
Hearts palpitate.
Fingers of sorrow caress the eyes
To a swollen weariness.

Why weep for the dead?
The eyes that weep
Next may be on Death's serial list.

In this dearth of gaiety
We long for death
For we cannot feign gaiety
When misery falls like rain
On our fragile hearts.

But weep not for the dead.
Bid farewell.
Wait for your time.

BAD AND HARD

He is a bad guy
Taking souls unawares
Leaving behind sorrows, tears
And a string of broken hearts.

He is a hard guy too.
Never gives an extra-time;
Often, not an iota of sign:
He comes to take, not to play.

A RUNNING LIFE
(FOR OSONDU)

His name was his life
And his life a path of thorns.
Osondu ran from birth
Racing through the misty
Narrow path of time.
Death flew after him
With a thousand knives at noon.
Death kept its chase
Into the dark dark side of life.

Time sighed.
Wind stood still.
Clouds froze.
And the sky possessed
Two suns at noon.
Death struck.

His soul walked gracefully
Through the gate of eternity
Made with shinning lights.

GOOD BYE, DEAR BROTHER (FOR JUDE)

I no longer write a dirge.
I have refused to remember
Your requiem mass.
I have refused to remind my soul
Of that dawn
When tears broke their barricades,
That painful dawn
When dark blanket of sorrow
Rolled out across my sky
Like sudden night at dawn.

I remind my soul
Of your laughter –
The sweet song of joy,
Of your words –
Soothing balm for my aching heart.

I honour the shining time
We shared together
Before you slowly walked away
Like a passing wind.
Good bye, brother,
Good bye!

FOUR
NIGERIA: IN THE MIDST OF MADNESS

The poems in this section are dedicated to the suffering masses in Nigeria. Since Nigeria, a country blessed with natural resources, got its independence in 1960, the country has been largely underdeveloped by her leaders. Nigeria supplies power to neighbouring countries, but within Nigeria there is constant power outage. There is no adequate supply of petroleum products, in spite of her being a major world supplier of crude oil, and liquefied natural gas. There is a near absolute decay of infrastructure. There is no quality health care. There is no quality education. Corruption is endemic and pervasive. And so on. Posterity shall judge every man's deeds, and someday, Nigeria, indeed Africa, shall arise.

THE POLITICAL RAPISTS

They built a paradise for us
And made a home for themselves.
They built a paradise with blocks of pain.
The roof is sealed with thick sorrow.
For fire we gather woods.
Their homes are made of metal and marble.
When the brook dries
We drink the waters from the clouds.
Their taps endlessly flow
Like God's abundant mercy.
We breathe air contaminated.
They inhale air conditioned,
Which is good for their glossy cheeks.
Our cheeks shrink like meat trembling
Before an aggressive fire that bites.
They call themselves the 'policy makers'.
We call them the 'public menace'.
We endure the pain of a raped election.
They enjoy the pleasures of a satisfied erection.
Our stomachs are filled with emptiness.
Did they expect us to vote with our lives?

A GHASTLY FUTURE

"Everyone is crying out for peace, and none is crying out for justice."
Peter Tosh

A ghastly future
Lies in the womb of history.
I seek no peace
In the dearth of justice.

A ghastly future
Lies in the womb of history.
Let's walk down the warpath,
Now we know
That these politicians
Perjured on the political pulpit.
Into their hands
We committed our coffers,
They chose to eat the bones
We hung around their necks,
Like rude dogs.
Yet there is peace!

A ghastly future
Lies in the womb of history
If blood be the prize
For equal right and justice
Let it be paid.

A ghastly future
Lies in the womb of history.
Even God planted on earth
No particular denomination

For man's liberation:
Mr. President, let the vintage man
Take your seat.
Fart, if you want to.
Don't feign refined manners.
They shroud the devil within.
I seek no peace,
And I see no peace,
In the dearth of justice.

A ghastly future
Lies in the womb of history.
Do we abort it:
Make the right choices now
And live in abundant peace and justice?
Or tend its birth
That peace may creep in
On stealthy feet – eventually?

PARADISE OF DECEIT

Without cease the people tithe their souls.
Without cease their lack lengthens.
Pastors preach prosperity on sacred pulpits,
Offer miracles with talisman,
Deep filthy fingers into God's pocket.

They offer a holy deceit,
Colonize the green minds of their followers
With the holy book of God:
Deceit is an art.

They say 'givers never lack'.
But neither give,
Nor explain our lengthening lack.
They say 'do not commit adultery'.
Night buries them between female thighs.

They say: 'thou shall not steal'.
They steal from God every Sunday.
'Thou shall not live on bread alone'.
They do not live on bread even.
Salads and marmalade work better for altered tastes.

But unlike the night that hides
Lust and its satiation,
The sun exposes the multi-million naira mansions,
The stainless listless ladies
At the back of their limousines and private jets.

Dear men of God,
I know God as a consuming fire too.
Someday an inferno shall strike your paper paradise.
And our eyes shall see the true miracle of the Lord.

BEFORE THE COURT OF CONSCIENCE

Unlike many great men
Whose names are preciously kept by History,
They do not strive
To make known their names to this sage – History.

They plunder from
The strengths of our heroes past.
Like petty thieves they steal
 From the defenceless.
These vagabonds in power (VIPs)
Set our dreams ablaze.

I bring you
Before the court of conscience
Let the judge of your introspection preside.
May truth prevail.

<u>FIVE</u>
CHAOS

It is time the human race grew beyond its weaknesses and learnt to resolve their differences through dialogue.

DELUSION

Heirs of hedonism we were.
A messy time
We had on earth.
While we lived
Liquor controlled many.
Some wooed women
For fleeting ecstasy.
Transgression seeped into many minds.
Unleashed our spirit
From the silver-cord
Unknowing of the path
It has to sail.
Now, silences fill the wind
At the crossroads on doomsday.

ARRIVAL AND DEPARTURE

War – death's disciple
Came in a canoe of violence,
Chased dialogue from the land,
Set men against themselves:
Foes fought friends, and foes.
Friends friends.

At the eleventh hour
Like a dove
Dialogue descended,
Cleaved the canoe of violence,
Killed war.
Fed men love
Arrayed them in harmony.

Now bliss fondles
The dawn of every man's life.

LOVERS IN PARADISE

Like lovers in paradise
They clung to each other,
A man and a woman,
Dreaming one dream,
Feeding their needs,
They lived one life.
On stealthy feet
Came a great fierce war,
Cleaved them abruptly apart,
Turned his flesh to dust.
A war with an empty meaning
Roughly rushed him beyond her touch,
And galled her gentle soul.

MEMORIES OF WAR

Memories of war
Tear my heart to shreds.
Unleash tears.
Chaos drowns my mind.
Yesterday's thoughts, resurrected,
Engulf the flowing tranquillity in my heart.
I am chastened.

NIGHT IS AN ACCESSORY

Night,
Armed with darkness,
Shelters many villains
Who take flight
At the sight of dawn's
Sudden surprise of sunlight.

WHY?

A drop of goodwill
Calms the stormy sea
In the dark world of the despised.
Now in a bright free world
They recompense the source
With a thousand bags of evil.
Why?

SIX
LOVE, LIFE, AND THE CELESTIAL

Some of the poems here are inspired by contemplations on the mysterious nature of The Sweet Absolute, The Absolute Reality, The Absolute Truth, Omnipresent, Omniscient and Omnipotent, which many call God. It is neither masculine nor feminine. It is formless, and Its love for soul is beyond words. The Sweet Absolute is nothing but love. And love itself is an act of worship. Love is life. And life, in spite of its numerous challenges, or even because of them, can be exciting, and fun. The other poems in this section dwell on love and life. And thus is the triangle complete: God, Love, Life.

SCHOOL OF LIFE

Life is a large school complex
Complete with kindergartens and universities.
Death and birth are the boatmen
Ferrying us to, and from, school.
Heaven is our true home.

THE SWEET ABSOLUTE

In solitude and silence,
In the stillness of my soul,
I commune with The Sweet Absolute.

I watch the wind
Run into a near-by church
For a short prayer to The Sweet Absolute.

Even nature knows.

SUN-WORSHIP

Again, the sun ascends to its throne of light.
Billions of leaves stretch out
In intense joy and gratitude.
As the leaves fill with sunlight,
With verve unabashed,
With power and passion in every pore,
They dance their gratitude in sun-worship.

MAD SUN

The sun wakes at dawn.
And dries the mists of dawn.
With what lust the sun blazes!

A mad sun.
Pretty nude.
Desperate to blaze
On the face of transparent clouds.

Noon.
Not exhausted, the sun.
Blaring through clouds
To stare a blazing, unblinking eye
Upon man on earth.
Singeing the toiling cloth of our bones.
Hyacinths wilt,
They bear not the hot vapour
Drifting out of the sea's million nostrils.
Insane is the sun.

WORSHIP

Come to me at night.
Let's occupy its silent side.
Hug, kiss, caress me!
The soft light
That flows from
Your luminous eyes
Exposes my emotions
To the staring stars
With arms akimbo in the sky.
Let's worship each other
In the shrine of love,
And flood each night
With subtle blue light.
Let dawn catch us together
With its shining eyes,
For I am not shy.
Adamma!
You are the rose
And in my heart you grow.
Romance me
Like the wind that
Romances the night's bald head.
Dwell in me and
I shall dwell in you, eternally.

EYES THAT BECKONED

I look into her alluring gaze,
I see the burning passion.
Pulled by the power of her gaze,
I let go of all fears
I surrender
In the temple of love.

HISTORY

History is the tale of a forgotten future.
The future is history yet unknown.
Tales with wings fly
Into dark hollow regions of history
Like bats desperate to dive into night's darkness,
They collapse into abeyance
Waiting for light to fall on them.
Oblivious we are of life
As fleeting drama.
If time crawls
And dusk never holds down dawn
With its shackles of darkness,
Into hollow regions of history
Every future falls and is forgotten.

ASHES TO ASHES, DUST TO DUST

Wisps of smoke from my
Burnt past
Hover around my present,
Like misty fog
In the face of dawn.
I walk into the shining
Future without fear
Knowing that I have
Burnt my past to ashes.
For ashes to ashes,
And dust to dust.

SIGHT BEYOND SIGHT

The future is not harmless.
It is armed with secret histories.
The man with perfect sight
Sees nothing beyond now.
The sightless diviner sees
The nakedness of tomorrow.

Like the sightless diviner
I wish to learn from blunders
That died with history,
And wait for the future like a sage.

THE URGE HAS REFUSED TO DIE (1)

I do not write
Because the time is right
But the urge to write
Has refused without reason to die.

In my dreams I write
Every night I write
Even if time is not right
And there is no light
But I have good sight
The urge knows I must write.

The urge has refused to die
And time seems to be always right
I cannot help but write
Because the urge has refused to die.

THE URGE HAS REFUSED TO DIE (2)

I desire so much to write,
But seldom know when time is right.
Now my ballpoint pen faces a paper.
Words cute and trim stagger out to wander,
Giving birth to themes which stoke my desire.
How I long to write and never retire!

A CACHE OF TRICKS

A crook
Fell into a brook
And broke
His back and neck.

Not long after
Along came another
Who thought himself smarter
Than the first or any other.

He came a man with a goal.
A cache of tricks he stole
From the crook that fell into the brook
And broke his back and neck.

But the cache fell from the crook
And fell into the brook.
It found a resting place
In the brook that gave no peace

To the crook that broke
His back and neck.
Thus was the cache of tricks
Lost to the crooks.

JAZZ

Jazz comes like wind
Filtering impurities
Driving me gently to the freedom I seek
Gradually, one after another, my thoughts die
The density fades
My soul glows
The fragrance of peace engulfs my soul
Still flowing with stability
Healing my sorrows and fragile emotions
Leaving behind an ineffable serenity
I am free, utterly

UNEARTHED BLISS
(FOR FELA)

Your songs burst
The frozen sorrow
On my soul's island.

Your songs seep
Into the pores of my soul
Like sunshine seeping
Into the pores of joyful leaves.

Your songs unearth,
At the core of my soul,
The buried bliss,
And stars fall off my eyes.

MY NIGHTS AND A NIGHTINGALE

Each dusk
Silence makes time seem still.
And I can hear lucid footfalls
Of receding wind.
As dusk deepens
And darkness takes charge
Sweet songs unwrap themselves
And clothe the night with peace.
Songs that soften even the devil's soul
Rush into my waiting ears
Like children rushing
For a father's embrace,
Caressing my soul
Like the wind romancing the rose,
Chasing loneliness away
Like great companions,
Leading me into shinning dreams
Like a great master.

Sing more, lone nightingale
O sing some more, bird of delight.
And may your songs
Also keep you company.

EPILOGUE

Let this urn gather my undying ashes
After what remains is burnt upon my death.

Soul is indestructible:
This urn shall bear my epitaph – still alive.

ABOUT THE AUTHOR

As a teenager, Nigerian born Chika Agbayi gained a place at Enugu State University of Science and Technology to study law. In 2004, he graduated from the university with an LL.B (Bachelor of Laws) and proceeded to the Nigerian Law School, Abuja, where he got his B.L (Barrister at Law) in 2007 and was subsequently called to the Nigerian Bar. After the compulsory one-year service to the nation, he left Nigeria for the United Kingdom where he studied for a few years. He holds a Master's degree in Business Administration from Heriot-Watt University Edinburgh, Scotland, United Kingdom. He lives and works in the United States of America.

www.ingramcontent.com/pod-product-compliance
Lightning Source LLC
LaVergne TN
LVHW040201080526
838202LV00042B/3265